Wanda L. Payne

Becoming Un-Mormon

Your Beliefs Hold the Key

THE
SELF
PUBLISHING
AGENCY

Wanda L. Payne
Becoming Un-Mormon: Your Beliefs Hold the Key

Imagine Publishing
Copyright © 2026 by Wanda L. Payne
First edition

Hardcover ISBN 979-8-9928761-0-9
Softcover ISBN 979-8-9928761-1-6
eBook ISBN 979-8-9928761-2-3

Book Design | Ashley Russell Designs
Editors | Justin Chevrier and Shelley Egan
Author Portrait Photographer | Brigham J. Taylor
Publishing Management | TSPA The Self Publishing Agency, Inc.

This book is dedicated to all those who feel they are not allowed to be their authentic selves and have yet to see that the ruby slippers are on their feet. They've had the answer all along.

Contents

Preface

I've heard the saying that everyone has a book inside them. About twenty-five years ago, a psychic told me that writing a book was part of my life path. I argued with her, saying that because I had absolutely no need to do that, it just would not happen. She really didn't care what my opinion was; she just said I would do it.

Fast-forward twenty-five years. Well, Barbara, you were right. I am being energetically "nudged" right now to tell my story. So why now and why this story? I just hope that it may help someone else on a similar journey of learning to accept oneself.

I am all about avoiding pain of any kind (last name notwithstanding). Especially trauma. Thirty years ago, I found myself on the precipice of changing my life forever. I was a very active member in the Mormon Church, and yet I found myself in love with another woman. I will use the term "Mormon" instead of the more formal term "The Church of Jesus Christ of Latter-day Saints" since it is shorter and more commonly known. It was terrifying to look over the edge of that cliff and imagine another way of living. I knew excommunication would be the next step for me because trying to live in two worlds was driving me crazy.

What I didn't know then was that my beliefs held the key. Mormons talk a lot about their testimony of the Church being of utmost importance. What this meant to me was that I was expected to believe all the Church's teachings.

I was struggling to own myself and to have peace of mind. I came to realize that my gut had to take precedence over my testimony. The gift I gave myself—without even realizing it at the time—was to believe in myself first. I figured no one could know what was better for me than I could. And since my core belief was that "Love Is It" (everything else is just everything else), I finally learned to trust my gut in all aspects of my life, figuring that I'd end up okay by sticking with that.

This book takes you on my transformational journey from being a superorthodox Mormon to being my true self and free to be me on every level.

Beginnings

The third of six siblings, I grew up in a very orthodox Mormon home. I was the peacekeeper, the middle child and a people pleaser to the core. I was raised very much "by the book." If there was a rule, I knew it and kept it. I went to all the meetings that were expected of me, kept the Word of Wisdom (a health code), dressed modestly and had only other Mormons for friends. I was baptized at eight years old (the standard age to be baptized), paid ten percent of any money I received for tithing, fasted on Fast Sunday (the first Sunday of each month) and took on any Church calling or job that was asked of me.

My grandfather was the temple president of the Mesa Arizona Temple in the forties and early fifties. At the time, it was the only temple in Arizona, Mexico, Nevada, New Mexico and California. Because of this, the leadership of the temple in Arizona was equivalent to being Mormon royalty. Many times, adults I had never met would find out my last name and immediately ask me if I was related to my grandfather. Once I confirmed that he was indeed my grandfather, they would go into raptures of how he had counseled them when they went to the temple and how he had saved their marriage. I don't know if this was common for other temple presidents' grandkids, but it was familiar enough for me.

My father held a high reverence for his father and wanted to raise his children righteously. The only sacrament meeting I remember missing as a child was when my older sister got stuck in the bathroom and couldn't get out. My dad eventually had to climb in through the small bathroom window and take the hinges off the door so that he could let her out. I never cared about attending sacrament meetings, so missing this one was no sacrifice. As an Institute instructor (someone who teaches classes for college-aged Mormons) once said, "It takes a great meeting to be better than no meeting at all." I feel that's true of all meetings, especially Church meetings, where one invariably hears the same thing on a weekly basis.

And there were many meetings to attend growing up, of course. They were all held at our Church buildings or at a learning institution. If you're Mormon, you know. But for those of you who don't, a quick summary of some of the meetings is as follows.

Daily

> »   Seminary: ninth- to twelfth-grade classes taken by students getting release time from regular high-school classes

Weekly

> »   Family Home Evening: all ages in each household
> »   Firesides: ages nineteen to thirty-five (could also be for other adults, but that varied)
> »   Institute: college-aged adult classes given at a college or university
> »   Priesthood Meetings: men aged nineteen to infinity and beyond
> »   Primary: children aged three to twelve
> »   Relief Society: women aged nineteen to infinity and beyond
> »   Sacrament Meetings: all ages
> »   Sunday School: all ages
> »   Ward Counsel Meetings: adults in leadership positions
> »   Young Adult Meetings: ages nineteen to thirty-five

» Young Women/Men: ages twelve to eighteen (includes Beehives: ages twelve to thirteen)

Monthly

» Home Teaching: two males who held the priesthood visited about four assigned homes
» Relief Society Visiting teaching: two women visited about four assigned homes

Every Six Months

» General Conference: all ages worldwide
» Stake Conference: all ages (See the list of Mormon terms for a definition of "stake.")

I know I've missed some, but what I'm trying to say—in the nicest possible way—is that there were a lot of meetings. I rarely missed any that were meant for me, and to think I would eventually be considered a rebellious or evil-seeking soul would have been absolutely laughable.

I bring this up because the belief in the Church at that time was that if you were a homosexual, you had made a conscious decision to be rebellious and to side with Satan or be evil. Now, I think the Church believes that if you are a homosexual, you made an agreement with Heavenly Father (God) before you came down to Earth. You would show how valiant you were by never acting on these horrible feelings that you had been given. To me, this is a very crazy-making assumption. It's like telling the left-handed person that the true way to God is never to use their left hand to write with or to do anything else, despite it being their dominant hand. I cannot even wrap my head around a God like that.

Another thing I had figured out by my early teens was that there were far worse things than being single. My parents barely knew each other a whole two weeks before they got married. Seriously. My dad had planned on going to Berkeley for law school and wanted my mother to come with him, so the only solution for good Mormon young adults was to get married. My mother was the only child of doting parents, and my dad was one of thirteen children who all pretty much had to fend for themselves. To say that my parents were on opposite ends of the universe is putting it mildly. For some reason, my mother chose to confide all the frustrations in her marriage to me. So, the gift I had from them was the message that being single was *way* better than being in a dysfunctional marriage. As a result, I just thought I was waiting for Mr. *Very* Right—Okay, Mr. Perfect!—in my twenties and thirties, in between all my Mormon meetings. I never once questioned anything more than that, as I was busy doing "what was expected" of me.

Love Is It

From an early age, I knew that love was essential in life. I seemed to have entered this life with the profound knowing that love is it. In my heart, I have always known that love is the highest law. Love is everything, and everything else is just everything else. All the meetings I attended stressed obedience more than love. I felt that, as a Church, we had abandoned Jesus's core message of love.

As a matter of fact, the only real argument I had in church happened when I was older. In a Sunday school class, I found myself arguing with the teacher that obedience was NOT the highest law; love was the highest law. The poor teacher who was assigned the task of teaching the class didn't know what to say to me, other than to read out of the lesson manual produced by the Church that plainly said obedience was at the top.

I don't remember exactly how old I was, but I would guess it was in my late twenties when I found myself totally disappointed with the "God the Father" idea of the God that I had been raised with. This God felt more to me like the God of the Old Testament. This seemed to take the Church back to the mentality of the Pharisees and Sadducees that Jesus dealt with. You know, the guys who counted how many steps they took on the Sabbath so they would know if they were righteous or condemned. (Hint: taking one step too many did not put you in a good place.) These were the guys who gave rise to Jesus's quote "The Sabbath was made for man, not man for the Sabbath" (Mark 2:27).

To me, the Pharisees and the Sadducees were on a "point system." By point system, I mean a system of arbitrary rules that could tell you exactly how righteous you were depending on what you did on the outside. Things like how valuable your sacrifice was based on the size and cost of it, which gave us the story of the widow's mite. Things like feeling entitled to stone the woman caught in adultery, which Jesus refuted by saying, "He that is without sin among you, let him first cast a stone at her." (John 8:7)

I grew up feeling like the Church operated on a similar point system. I know they don't actually call it a point system, but the understanding that paying tithing (also jokingly called "fire insurance"); serving an honorable mission (which includes paying for any of your children's missions); being an Eagle Scout if you're a male; getting married in the temple to a person of the opposite sex; obeying your husband's decisions (assuming he's a worthy priesthood holder—and who gets to decide that?); going to the temple regularly; visiting teaching or home teaching regularly; receiving the home teachers; accepting all Church callings; and so on are important to do if you want to reach the highest part of the celestial kingdom, the tip-top of heaven. So, if all the above and more are important to Heavenly Father when it comes time to judge whether you are worthy of going to the celestial kingdom, I would say that all Mormons operate on a point system.

If you were only baptized but not active in the Church, woe be unto you because you had the chance to be active in this life but didn't use the time you had here righteously. And even worse, if you were a member of the Church but were excommunicated for whatever reason and were not rebaptized, you would be in outer darkness: true and utter hell. The thought is that you knew better because you were baptized—and who at age eight doesn't know better—but deliberately chose to side with Satan.

Since I mentioned that filling an honorable mission is important to your heavenly standing, I thought I'd mention my brother David's experience. My brother realized that he was gay before he got his mission calling. All honorable men went on a two-year mission for the Church when they were eighteen or nineteen years old. He was worried about going on his mission and being homosexual and talked to his bishop about it. His bishop told him that if he served an honorable mission, he wouldn't have those feelings anymore. And let me tell you that there was no missionary who worked harder on his mission than my brother David. He was highly motivated to fulfill a superhonorable mission.

But when he came back, he still felt attracted to men. He had a new bishop by this time, and he talked to that bishop about his feelings. That bishop told him that if he fulfilled another mission—a stake mission— honorably, all those horrible feelings would go away. A stake mission is conducted while you still live at home, where you teach people who are interested in hearing more about the Church. A regular mission, which you do when you're eighteen or nineteen, is always someplace far away. David's first mission had been in Germany.

So when he was going to Arizona State University (ASU) to do his premed schooling, he put in all the hours it would take to do a stake mission, usually at least ten hours a week. Even after all this extra effort, he realized that all the "missioning" in the world was not going to change his sexual identity, despite what his bishops had promised.

When the second mission didn't work, my brother decided to submit himself to shock therapy at Brigham Young University. This was not a cheap solution nor was it easy on his psyche, but he was serious about his desire to be a worthy member of the Church. While there he went through the therapy of being electrically shocked every time they showed him a picture of a man, dressed or undressed. After a few days of this, he pulled one of the counselors aside to talk. He said, "I get that you are building up an aversion in me towards men. But what do you plan to do to create in me an attraction towards women?" The counselor said, "Well, if you're not attracted to men, of course you'll be attracted to women. They'll be your only sexual outlet left." My brother said, "I see." He thought, *He's crazier than I am*. He promptly went to his room, packed up his belongings and left.

Back to my disappointment in the "God the Father" idea of God, I thought that the Mormon version of God was very possibly one of the gods out there but couldn't be the only one. After all, where did he come from? I also thought—I tend to do a lot of thinking—that gods probably got their power (at least part of it) from our worship of them. From us, in fact.

You may be unaware that this was very radical thinking for an orthodox Mormon. Despite that, at the end of my thinking, I realized there was only one thing left for me to do. I had to replace this Mormon God with a better one.

Then I had to think about what attributes I would expect of my God. My God had to be unconditionally loving, compassionate, funny, kind, patient, nonjudgmental, and incredibly wise. So, in my mind, it was simple—I had to fire the Mormon God and replace him with my new and improved God. Since my God would be so awesome and nonjudgmental, our relationship would only get stronger over time.

I have since realized that if you feel your God is constantly judging you, or will even wait to judge you at the end of your life, it creates distance. Even if you trust your God to judge you fairly, there's always the element of feeling that parts of you might be lacking.

Instead of feeling like we need God to judge us, I feel like we have picked the classes we're taking in schoolroom Earth. Since we've chosen the challenges we are to experience on Earth, we will know if we have gotten the lesson we came here to learn. If we do not learn what we chose, we can come back to Earth and take the class again. If we have learned it, we're done with that lesson.

I never told anyone about my shift in allegiance, but changing my God helped me sleep better at night. I didn't realize it then, but this was a huge step towards unraveling the major programming that had started with me before I was even born.

The Setup

I started my career in accounting at age sixteen, when I worked for a printing company between my junior and senior years of high school. During my senior year, I had released time for half of my day and continued at the printing company—in areas such as accounts payable, accounts receivable, and payroll—for the rest of my day. While working for that company, I took some accounting courses from Mesa Community College, where everything in the accounting arena came together in my head.

From there I worked for a general contractor. I continued to expand my accounting knowledge and started working on a computer system that we accessed via shared time on a telephone line. I really got comfortable with the accounting field during this time. When my boss eventually sold his business, I became an independent contractor, helping other general contractors while looking for work.

At thirty-five, I was hired as the CFO at a small commercial-cabinet company. This was very exciting because, for the first time, I felt respected and valued as a woman. Being seen and valued totally changed my world. At that time, computers were just entering the small-business arena. I was also in charge of creating "the books," or how the books would be structured on software that we shared via the telephone.

I tell you this not to impress upon you how important I was, nor how old I am, but rather to help you understand what an exciting time this was for me. In the Mormon arena, women are the supporting members of the Church. White men run the show. After all, they have the priesthood. So that you understand, it was huge for me, as a valued and respected woman, to be in the position of CFO in a predominantly white-male Mormon company. It was just part of my programming as a woman that I expected to be more of a supportive staff member instead of a valued asset with professional opinions that were actually heard and valued.

When I started working there, they already had a receptionist-office manager named Ellen, a front-office staff, and a back-office team.

As time passed, Ellen and I talked at work, and I learned that she had recently moved from Utah, where she had gone to school and fallen in love with her female roommate, Jackie. They were both Mormon, and their relationship had been discovered and reported to their bishop. He called them in, read them "the riot act," and threatened to excommunicate them if a practicing homosexual relationship happened again. For those of you who are unfamiliar with the Mormon religion, it—much like other organized religions—considers same-sex relationships to be evil and absolutely not tolerated.

Jackie believed the bishop and determined that her relationship with Ellen was over. She moved to Arizona to find work to put distance between them. Ellen still had feelings for Jackie, though, so she followed her to Arizona and found work at the cabinet shop about six months before I was hired.

Since Ellen and I worked together in the front office, we would sometimes talk about personal stuff. Quite often, she would tell me about the angst she was experiencing about Jackie, who treated her like a friend but not a lover. Once in a while, we would go to my house, watch *Anne of Green Gables*, and eat canned Chinese food, though I daresay the Chinese would totally disown what we called "chow mein." We had time to relax together and gradually became friends. But there was always this theme of how much Ellen was still in love with Jackie. We'd also talk about how Jackie just wouldn't be with Ellen because of her fear that if she were, she would lose her God connection if she were to be excommunicated.

Ellen was on a women's Church softball team, and I would watch her play. When she didn't go home for the holidays, she would come to my family gatherings. We went to some evening social events and just got comfortable doing little things together. Things went on like this for probably nine months until, one day, I realized I had more than "just friends" feelings for Ellen.

That's when what I call the "wasps" started. A deep-down feeling of wasps buzzing around and stinging me inside started up. This feeling was there all day, and it woke me up many nights. Thinking back, it not only reminded me of wasps but also felt like getting a low-grade electrical shock 24/7. It was not an actual physical thing but felt very emotional. I really didn't know what the core issue was. I was so clueless. The only reason I could think of regarding why I was experiencing this feeling of "wasps" was that I was emotionally attached to Ellen, and I had determined that I could never tell her how I felt. To me, it was clearly hopeless to tell her because she was still in love with Jackie.

Also, I'd had my parents as role models, and so I was in no hurry to marry anyone, like ever. So I was pretty shocked to find myself—at the age of thirty-six—not only having a crush, but having a crush on a girl.

Being gay is taboo in many societies, but it's even more taboo when you're in a high-profile position in the Young Women's Organization of the Mormon Church, which I held at the time. This was the other reason why I had determined that I could never tell Ellen how I truly felt.

Testimony

During the "wasps" phase, I was trying to do anything that would give me some peace. It had me seeking solace on mountain tops overlooking the valley in the Phoenix area. They weren't Everest, so you needn't be impressed. The mountains was just someplace to go away from everyone so I could try to unravel my emotions. I also attended random ball games, sitting in the bleachers among strangers. This allowed me to be around people while still feeling alone to work through my feelings. There were times during this phase when I would wake up at two-thirty in the morning and realize that there was no getting back to sleep. The wasps never slept. The emotional angst I was in just wouldn't turn off. So, I would go grocery shopping at three in the morning. I quickly realized that this was a pretty great time to go grocery shopping. The shelves were being stocked so there was a lot to choose from and there were no lines at checkout. As convenient as it was to get the weekly grocery shopping done quickly, I would have done anything to stop the wasps.

I even visited the temple in downtown Mesa to participate in "sessions," hoping to find some relief from the wasps. To provide more context, I had gone through the temple for the first time a few years prior, in my early thirties. My initial temple experience was very traumatic for my own personal reasons. Because of that, I swore to myself that I had done "what was expected of me" and would never go again—under any circumstances.

I had never even thought about going back until the wasps started happening. The point is, I would have considered doing almost anything to get rid of them, including going back to the temple, despite how traumatic the experience had been for me. That pretty much sums up how painful and stressful the wasps feeling was. Temple sessions became something to do and were okay at this point in my life. They were quiet and relatively peaceful, providing me with an activity. However, even these sessions did nothing to stop the wasps.

What helped me the most was going to Sedona on Saturday mornings, at about ten. Upon arrival, I would find a fast-food drive-through and get a sandwich.

Then I would head to Oak Creek, find a place to scramble down and sit on the creek's banks. Watching and listening to the water go by while munching on my sandwich, I could feel the energy of the creek wash through my whole being, bringing healing and peace. It was absolutely wonderful. I'd sit there for a couple of hours before driving the two hours back home. This would calm the wasps for a day or so, but inevitably, they would return.

I even tried playing mind games by completely ignoring Ellen and not talking to her at work for several days. My goal was to create some emotional distance. However, she would become concerned and start asking, "Are you okay?" or "Are you feeling sad? What's wrong with you?" I continued playing mind games for quite some time but could never make it stick!

I even seriously considered quitting my job: Ellen and I worked together every day so there was no way to create emotional distance from her. As you know, I loved my job like I never had before. It hurt my heart to even think of quitting, but the wasps were unrelenting.

Another reason I didn't quit was because I couldn't think of what to tell the boss. "I have to quit because I'm in love with the receptionist" was true. He was a very conservative Mormon, though, and it didn't seem like I could tell him that. Besides, I'm a terrible liar. If I'd made up another reason, he would have known I was lying just by looking at me.

The wasps went on for a couple of years. Then one night, I went to the junior high to walk around their track. I was walking around and around by myself. And I yelled in my mind, "Okay, God. What do you want me to do to get the wasps to go away?" The answer I received was clear and to the point. The directive was to "just tell Ellen how you feel." Obviously, I was shocked by this answer, and like so many people would, I yelled out loud, "NO WAY!" And the wasps continued their incessant stinging.

After about two more months of the wasps, I caved in and followed the directive I had been given. To use Mormon vernacular, when I told her how I felt—in love—I had a strong "testimony," or belief, that this step was hugely important in my life. I'd fought it with everything that I had for two years. When I finally quit resisting and told Ellen how I felt, like magic, all the wasps inside me relaxed and went to sleep. No more buzzing and stinging.

So, I'm a Lesbian?

Things didn't turn out well. In response to my declaration of love, Ellen just said, "I seem to ruin everyone's life." That was definitely not what I had expected, but in retrospect, she was probably referring to Jackie and me. We were both Mormons, and Ellen likely thought that my getting involved with her would ruin our lives. At least the wasps were sleeping. As Martha Beck, the life coach, was fond of saying, it's best to "cave early." So sleep, wasps. Sleep.

I don't remember my exact response to Ellen's odd comment, but it was probably something brilliant like "Okay." I didn't have a snappy comeback, but the beauty of the moment was that the wasps were gone! And I mean truly gone, for the first time in a couple of years! Amazing! I was grateful and a bit blown away.

The wasps were so completely gone that I didn't care about the relationship, quitting my job, or anything else. I felt like myself again, until a couple of months later when Ellen told me she was going back home the following month, out of state, to visit her family. She said she'd be gone for a week . . . which happened to be the exact same week as my birthday. But she went on to say that she could be gone for either the week of my birthday or Jackie's, and that she had decided to be here for Jackie's birthday.

To say that I was hurt and mad would be an understatement, and it just totally shut me down emotionally, especially since I had just shared my feelings with her. Despite that, it was somehow okay to be gone for my birthday but not for Jackie's. That really showed me that Jackie was still her first priority. Ellen went on to assure me that she hadn't forgotten my birthday, as she had asked Jackie to drop off a present for me while she was gone. I didn't say anything but thought to myself, *You know what? We're done.* So I told her not to bother and that I didn't need Jackie to drop off anything. For the first time in several years, I didn't care if I ever saw Ellen again. She was clearly unaware of how I felt as she continued just as though nothing had happened between us.

Now by this point, dear reader, you may be asking yourself, "Wanda, why didn't you tell her how much this upset you and to buzz off?" Remember, I was the "peacekeeper," and I realized that we still had to work together every day. She did clearly tell me—without telling me—that I was not her priority: Jackie was. In my mind, this meant that there was nothing I could do about it. It was what it was.

While we continued to work together every day, there was a little bit of distance between us, for me anyway. We spoke about work-related things for the most part. I was done with any notions that there was or could be an "us." Then it came time for her trip back home to visit family. While she was gone, she called me frequently, and of course, I talked to her politely. I tend to be chronically polite. But the hurt I felt and the absence of wasps made me indifferent to her calls. I was over it. Something inside me had snapped, and I was done.

When Ellen returned, she wanted to walk around the track together again one evening after work. Part of me thought, *Well, I guess she can still be a friend. She will just never be my person.* We drove separately to the track and walked together. She told me about her trip, and I just listened quietly. As we were going to our cars, she said she had missed me.

I said, "Okay."

And then she said, while looking me straight in the eyes, "No, I mean I *really* missed you."

I knew she was saying that she had more than just-friends feelings for me as well.

Well, by then I didn't care. I wasn't emotionally involved at that point, and for the first time, I had a decision to make: jump into the relationship or stay out. I thought of all the temple sessions, hiding in plain sight at ball games, hiking up mountains, and especially Sedona and Oak Creek.

If there was one thing I had a strong testimony of, it was that God had played me. I could run from this relationship, but I couldn't hide. For some unexplainable reason, this relationship had been factored into my life unbeknownst to me. Being the orthodox Mormon that I was, I figured the relationship would last . . . maybe three months. It had taken a long time to get this far, and I had no illusions that Ellen was really over Jackie.

But after all that thinking, even though I thought I was done with the relationship, I made a clear and cold decision to throw my lot in with Ellen's and see what lessons were in store for me. Ahhhhh, the innocence of youth! We were both living the "active Mormon" life. For us, that meant no sex or kissing when we first got together. But we did lots of hugging. When we hugged, I had a huge feeling of "I'm home." And there wasn't a particle of evil in it. Just peace, and frankly, it doesn't get better than that—especially to a recent exterminator of wasps. I didn't know everything about love or even sin, but I knew it didn't feel "righter." If you let others dictate how you feel, you are well and truly ready for therapy.

A patriarchal blessing is a blessing that you get from the stake patriarch, which is to be a guide throughout your life. I had gotten mine at the age of twelve. It had warned me to be cautious of evil friends in my youth. Because of that, I had always worried that I'd be sucked into some den of iniquity. Would I know evil if it came up to me? I had been preached to in Church to think that "those homosexuals" were evil and even an abomination to God. Not an irritation, but a real and true abomination. That's pretty harsh. And at the time, of course, anyone who was a "practicing (as if we need to practice?!) homosexual" had deliberately chosen that behavior just to be rebellious or evil. Okay, that is not my description.

I had gay friends growing up, but they were not evil to me. They never tried to "convert" me. They were just "wired" differently than I was. They were what I considered "Christian" or kind and giving people. There were no sexual covens, no rites of passage—just a feeling from them that they were not allowed to be authentic. Or society would stone them to death. I was sad for them but not sexually attracted to them.

On a night reasonably soon after our reconciliation, while driving home from Ellen's apartment, I had the following conversation in my head. "I'm in love with a woman. Well, I'll be. That makes me a lesbian. Who knew?"

My older brother said he always knew—but he didn't know for sure. I just assumed that I was straight but that I was waiting for the "perfect man," whatever that was. After my parents' miserable marriage and my firm belief that there are far worse things than not being married, I just figured that maybe I'd be single for life. I'm glad my response to myself wasn't one of horror or fear. Instead, my reaction was just a very matter of fact. "Well, if this, then that." This unemotional response made that part more straightforward. And by the way, I was thirty-eight at this time.

I figured our relationship would only last a few months, and that at worst, we would be disfellowshipped and brought to repentance at the end of that time.

Authenticity

When our relationship started, I had led the Beehives (twelve- to thirteen-year-old girls in our ward) for about four years. Since integrity was such a freaking big deal to me, I felt guilty about being their leader. Several years prior, I'd made myself go through the temple so I could wear garments—special Mormon religious underwear—so parents would know that their kids had an excellent example of a leader.

Mormons know that you're wearing garments because the outline of the underwear is slightly visible through the outer clothing. For example, if you're a nonreligious guy who has a button-down white dress shirt on and is wearing an undershirt, people can see that outline under the dress shirt. Wearing garments is basically the same concept, but instead of an under-shirt, the garments from the temple are our underwear.

During the summer, I went with the Beehives to camp. Our ward had enough Beehives to fill a cabin, and I was the cabin mom. One night one of the girls saw a spider while we were all in bed, and she had a fear of spiders, as most girls do. She started crying and was getting more emotional by the minute. I could see the whole cabin starting to copy her energy: most of the girls were starting to whimper and cry. I did the only thing I could think of, and that was to crawl into her bunk with her. I told her I would stay until she felt safe. Her hysterics immediately stopped, and the whole cabin was soon asleep. As soon as she calmed down, I got back into my bunk. As a leader, it was a good move, but I couldn't help wondering how the girls and their parents would judge that action if they knew that I was gay.

Speaking of the Beehives, as their leader, I taught them lessons each week and did activities with them a couple of times a month. But each time I stood up in front of them to teach them a Church lesson, I felt like a fraud. We did fund-raising—washed cars, sold candy bars, and did bake sales—in order to go to camp. After realizing I was gay, I was always very aware that I was not what the girls—or, more particularly—their parents would approve of as their leader.

At that time, Ellen was Relief Society president in her Young Adult ward. We were both very concerned with appearances, and it drove me crazy that we had to be. When I'd go to the Gay section at the Changing Hands Bookstore, I'd slump down and hope no one saw me. It was cloak-and-dagger time, and I hated feeling inauthentic. But I thought this was going to be a short phase. Little did I know.

Right after Ellen and I got together, we were on a high. I have since learned it's called "limerence." I remember one night, as we were leaving TGIFs after dinner, how happy we both were. I remember asking her how long this phase lasted. Remember, she'd had Jackie as a first love, so she was "experienced." She said she didn't know. I told her probably not more than a few months.

She responded, "As if you know everything. What would make you say such a silly thing?" I just said I figured it would kill people if it lasted much longer. That did make her laugh!

We also just went on regular dates, like to the movies or to other fun events. But after all these years, the thing that stands out in my mind the most is how it felt to just hold her. The feeling of "I'm home" was so very comforting and amazing.

And Then There's Mom

As I've mentioned already, my parents' dysfunctional marriage gave me a unique perspective—even for a Mormon—on relationships and life in general. To better understand my parents' marriage, not only was my father one of thirteen children, but my grandfather was idolized by the adults in my dad's life even though he never provided for his family in any great measure. That left my grandmother with the responsibility to do anything she could to keep a roof over their heads and food on the table. My father was also raised in an era in which children were to be seen but not heard. That meant there was never any real conversation or interaction between my grandfather and his children until they had all reached adulthood.

My mother, on the other hand, was raised by parents who married relatively late in life—at twenty-three and twenty-five—and tried throughout their whole marriage to have children. Finally, when my grandmother was about thirty-nine, she got pregnant. This was a true miracle baby. When my mother was born, she was rather frail, and both of her parents became the original helicopter parents. They never felt sure that she would survive to live another day. They told her how they would sit over her crib just for the joy of watching her breathe.

My grandmother got pernicious anemia when my mother was young, and as the disease progressed, she lost all function of her arms and legs. By the time my mother was twelve, her mother was a quadriplegic, and her father had to care for both his wife and his daughter. Far from living out the old adage that "children should be seen but not heard," her father was an excellent mom-dad. My mother recounted to me how he had her friend over to their house the day before Easter to dye Easter eggs. Then her friend was invited to come over for breakfast the next morning. After eating, they looked all over the yard for the Easter eggs he had hidden.

My grandfather, who adored his only daughter, had a job with the state of Arizona's tax commission. He got up every weekday morning and walked ten minutes or so to Central from their home in Phoenix in his required three-piece suit, tie and hat. Then he took the trolley to the state capital. He worked there until he retired in 1950. The Depression was hard on everyone, but at least he had a reliable way to provide for his family even during those times.

I knew that my mother was spoiled by her adoring parents. I once asked her if she thought that she was spoiled. She said absolutely NOT. I asked her why she thought that. She said that when she was growing up, her parents deliberately did not buy her everything she wanted so she wouldn't be spoiled. Her answer didn't convince me.

So, here was a woman who was obviously spoiled growing up, now living with a man who wasn't taught to be motivated to provide for us. But he said he had to work late every night. One night a friend of his, seeing that my father's light was on, went by his office to talk to him. He found him sitting in his chair reading the *Reader's Digest* magazine. The next time my father's friend saw my mom, he teased her, saying that she must be hard to live with because my dad preferred reading magazines at the office to being home with us. That created lots of friction between my parents. My mom thought that he could either help her with the kids or make a decent living. He did neither even though he passed the bar and practiced law for a while before going back to school and getting certified as a CPA. He wanted to be like his dad so much that he couldn't bring himself to bill anyone for his services. A temple president is expected to devote all his time to the Church, so he was paid by the Church for his services.

My dad died when I was twenty-four years old, and I could feel the prison doors of my own home slam shut. Better than anyone else in the family, I knew what my mom expected of me. She relied on my consistent income to help keep everything running her way. Also, my younger sister and brother were just fifteen and thirteen, and I was expected to help finish raising them.

By the time Ellen entered the picture, my younger siblings were adults and gone from the house, but I knew that my mom still had huge expectations of me. Nothing had happened during the ensuing fourteen years to make her any less spoiled.

Over the next five years, as our relationship continued, Ellen was living about two miles from me in her apartment, and I was living with my mom in her house. Why, you ask, weren't we living together? We had been together for five years already and were obviously a couple in our own eyes. If I had married a man, my mom could have dealt with me leaving her. But in her eyes, because I hadn't come out to her or anyone else in my family at that time, I was still single. And I was the people pleaser. I knew that she, like so many other parents, wouldn't understand why her daughter would abandon her in order to be deliberately evil. But since I clearly wasn't going to marry a man—because I was already married in my mind and heart to Ellen—my mother continued to expect complete fidelity.

During this time, I was obviously struggling with my identity, as you can imagine, and went to a therapist. After a number of sessions, he eventually asked me why I was still living with my mom. I simply told him, "To make her happy." He said, "I see. So, is she happy?"

When I thought about the question, I came to realize that she wasn't a happy person. That was a big aha moment for me. I'd never really realized that my living with her was not making her happy. She liked being well taken care of, and I was the "husband" she wished she'd had on every level but one. I took care of the house and even brought her flowers for no particular reason. But even that didn't really make her happy.

At that time—I was forty-two—I made a mental note that said at least one of us should be happy. And in response to his question, I said, "No, she's not happy." When my therapist asked his original question again, it took me a while to process. Then I realized that there was nothing but guilt holding me there. Needless to say, when Ellen and I did finally move in together—three years after this conversation with my therapist—my mom was furious. Our moving in together was an ending for her but a whole new beginning for us.

General Conference

After Ellen and I had been together for about four years, I was given the Church position of Young Women's president in my ward. This meant that I was over the entire Young Women's organization (twelve-to eighteen-year-old girls). Two counselors and a secretary helped me, but the position I held was very labor intensive. I taught weekly lessons to the sixteen-to eighteen-year-olds and helped create activities that they would like. As leaders we also wanted to have activities that would be more than fun and games. We looked for things to do that included some element of community service.

Now I really had all eyes on me. Whenever I went to general conference (to a stake center), Boyd K. Packer, president of the Quorum of the Twelve Apostles, would inevitably give a talk. The only topic he seemed capable of discussing was homosexuality. I think he gave the same talk every time, but he became a little more condemning as time passed.

In 1992, the last time I heard President Packer talk, he was saying that being a homosexual was not a "lifestyle." It was, in fact, a heinous crime against God. Now, I got curious about the definition of "heinous," and so I looked it up. It includes such things as murder, assault, rape, kidnapping and arson. You'd be shocked to know that this was the last general conference I submitted myself to. I can only suppose that little speech was to bring us homosexuals to repentance. You can't repent of how you are wired any more than you can repent of being a Black person or being a blonde. But I've read that his talks lead to a rise in suicides for the homosexuals in the Church.

Some souls felt dead inside after his talk, and I was one of them. Now, THAT is truly a heinous crime against God and all his children. It sets a dangerous precedent, making members of the Church feel justi-fied in judging others harshly. Families with homosexual people in them become fractured: parents disown children, siblings disown each other, and children disown parents. This fragmentation under-mines the supposed sanctity of the family unit in the Mormon Church. Heinous indeed. However, I had to credit Boyd K. That general conference was the last I ever attended, and without his "understanding and compassion," it might have taken me longer to see the light.

My People

The situation at home with my mom wasn't getting easier, even after four years of dating Ellen. Thankfully, I had my older brother David to help navigate it. Knowing that I was struggling with being gay and being in the Church, he suggested that I attend a meeting of a group called Affirmation. He explained that it was a group of Mormons supporting gay and lesbian members. I felt hopeful, thinking these might be "my people." We attended a few meetings together.

I remember that they announced Carol Lynn Pearson would be a guest speaker at the next meeting. I was excited because she had written a book—*Goodbye, I Love You*—about her story of divorcing her gay husband. And when he got AIDS, she took him in to nurse him until he died. She came and spoke at the next event. All the gay Mormons I knew of heralded her as a hero because she showed compassion instead of revulsion when faced with caring for someone with

AIDS. I got the odd feeling that she wasn't there to support the gay factor of the Church as much as she was there to show how to take the high road. We really didn't care because she was a known Church celebrity, as a poet, and we loved her.

I can't recall any other specific discussions, but I do remember feeling an overwhelming sadness and darkness. I am sensitive to the energy of others, and the atmosphere just felt somber, with people appearing bitter, sad, depressed, angry, ashamed, or just plain miserable. I quickly realized that the members of this group were not my people. And I thought, *Maybe this is what it looks like when you lose the gift of the Holy Ghost.*

Mormons are told that when they are baptized, they are given the gift of the Holy Ghost, and that when they are excommunicated, the gift is taken away. To Mormons, this gift is our "God connection." According to the Church, the only way to get that gift back is to get back into the Church by getting rebaptized. Without that connection, I, too, might look like the folks at that meeting. Serious thoughts, indeed.

I had another thought. What if these people were downers because they felt rejected? What if they felt rejected not only by their "Mormon second family" (the ward or congregation they live in), but probably by their families of origin, friends, and most importantly, by their God too? That couldn't leave people in a good mood; rather, they would probably be very angry and depressed.

And finally I thought, what if my feelings about getting excommunicated were that I felt it was the best thing to ever happen to me? What if the absolute freedom to be me was so liberating that I was thrilled to be out of the pretending? What if I felt like this was the coolest thing ever? And when this thought settled in, I knew without a doubt that I'd be fine. And I knew I would not be like "those people."

By this time, I was very weary of living the duplicitous life I had been living. Also, I was still in love with Ellen, and the notion that my love for her would last just three months had long since faded. I don't think I fully realized it at the time, but I was mentally and emotionally preparing to be excommunicated.

In that moment, I didn't realize why I felt a peace and calm fall over me. I just knew that if I could change my beliefs about being excommunicated, I'd be fine. I didn't realize it at the time, but firing my old God was hugely important. Any church can say they have the ability to sever someone's God connection—such as to take away the Holy Ghost—but it cannot do that. It would take me *believing* that the Church could break that connection to break it. And the last thing my God wanted was to stop interacting with me. And since my God was very cool and pretty funny, it's the last thing I wanted too.

Since I knew that love is it, of course my God knew that too. If love truly is it, loving someone else is brilliant, even if she is the same gender. Love is it, and everything else is just everything else.

I knew that my God was totally nonjudgmental. I have since come to believe that judging ourselves or others is the number one stumbling block to people's progression in this lifetime. It does no good and keeps us from totally loving ourselves and others. And since love is it, why would we be okay with blocking love from anyone?

My older brother, David, was a brilliant physician. He practiced medicine when the AIDS epidemic was in full swing. He doctored many HIV-positive men. And he would visit many who were in the hospital in their last hours. Several had been raised in very religious homes. All too often, those guys would hang on and suffer much longer than they should have because they were terrified of dying. They had been taught that, for being gay, they would burn in hell for eternity. David would try to tell them they had been taught nonsense, but they wouldn't listen. It always broke his heart to see them so wasted physically and so very terrified. My God never judges, and nor should we.

I also knew that my God was all about integrity and authenticity. Living the lie I had been for the past five years was killing me. I love Brené Brown, who tells us that the only way we can really be known to anyone is by doing the brave thing and being authentic. Most people are terrified to be themselves. But for me, terrified or not, that was my only option.

And I'm going to be totally authentic here and tell you that I was very terrified. I was such a pleaser. So when I tell you that you get to believe whatever you want, please try to change your beliefs to whatever will bring you peace. When you find peace, hang onto it, my friend.

The First Domino

When Ellen and I started our relationship, my Church position was leader over the twelve- to thirteen-year-old girls, and she was Relief Society president in the singles' ward. Time passed and I was given the position of Young Women's president in our ward, which I held for three years. Ellen timed out of her position as Relief Society president in the singles' ward and was assigned to her home ward, where she taught in the Primary.

I share this with you so you know how very involved I was with the Church, holding high-profile positions in the Young Women's organization. With that came a lot of responsibility. As much as I enjoyed these positions, ultimately, the dichotomy of it all left me feeling emotionally drained and stressed out, constantly feeling like I would be "found out" at any moment and turned in to my bishop. As someone who places a high value on integrity and authenticity, I was finding it increasingly difficult to be authentic in a place where being authentic would get me not only excommunicated but also ostracized by the same people for whom I was a role model.

During this time, Ellen had a moment of indiscretion. During her visiting teacher's visit, Ellen confided in her that she was gay. Well, it barely took twenty minutes after that visiting teacher left before Ellen received a phone call from her bishop. Word travels fast. He told her he needed to meet with her right away. She knew exactly why and dutifully went in the next day to meet with him. He wanted to know if what he had heard was true. He wanted to know if she was a homosexual, if she was still with that person—or, in other words, practicing—or if she had repented and dumped that person.

When Ellen admitted she was still with her partner, he started questioning her about our relationship. He demanded to know her partner's name. When she asked why he needed that, he said that my bishop would need to be notified. When she wouldn't give him my name, he said she had to. She asked him why again, and he said there was a spot on the form that asked that question and the form had to be completely filled out. To her credit, she wouldn't divulge that information.

Ellen's bishop decided she could be saved since she was young and attractive, so he decided to disfellowship her for the next twelve months. And so, as part of her disfellowshipment, she started a year of probation with special monthly meetings with the bishop. The meetings were versions of "good ol' Boyd K. Packer" talks. The bishop would quote scripture and read Church doctrine that made her feel lower than snail slime. When she would leave his office on the evenings that she went in to him, she would be depressed. Every meeting was the same: spiritual and emotional abuse at its heaviest. Of course, her bishop felt justified because it was his job to break her spirit into repenting unto God.

After about six months of this, I told her I didn't want her to go back to submit herself to the same cruelty she kept facing. She felt they would excommunicate her if she didn't attend those monthly meetings. Finally, I'd had it. I told her that if she went to this meeting one more time, I would go with her and tell that bishop he wouldn't be seeing her again.

Ellen said, "If you do that, he'll know who you are and notify your bishop."

I said, "I really don't care. I won't stand by for this abuse one more time."

That seemed to penetrate her fog of fear, and she quit going to the floggings. If you're invited to a flogging, just say *no*.

Time went on and Ellen's year of probation was coming to a close. All you are allowed to do is sing in the choir and attend sacrament meetings if you're being disfellowshipped. By this point, I had been released as Young Women's president and given the calling of second counselor in the Relief Society presidency. Ellen's bishop had decided she wouldn't shape up and it would be pointless to call her to repent. He had decided it was time to excommunicate her.

Getting Answers

Since Ellen was coming up on her year of being disfellowshipped and would be excommunicated very soon, I was really intent on getting answers to my own prayers as to whether I should turn myself in to my bishop for being gay. Since the Church didn't have cameras in every bedroom, they relied on you to turn yourself in, or risk being turned in by someone who had heard something about you, like Ellen's visiting teacher.

In the Mormon Church, the first Sunday of every month is called Fast Sunday. It's when everyone is supposed to go without food—to fast—or anything but water and to donate their savings from the twenty-four hours of fasting to the Church to give to the poor. You are also supposed to have a purpose in mind when you do this, and you are supposed to pray about it. My purpose for the past twelve months on Fast Sunday was to ask in prayer, "Is now the time that I turn myself in to my bishop for being a practicing gay person?"

The fasting was supposed to put you in a more spiritual mode so you could get answers. If I'm being totally honest, all the fasting did was make me very hungry and, consequently, rather grumpy. I never did get the spiritual aspect of it. But I did see that if you had a purpose for your suffering, which fasting was to me, maybe it wouldn't seem like such a waste.

A mysterious thing to me is that the Church emphasizes personal revelation. However, when your inspiration differs from that of the Church, you're expected to disregard your inspiration. Reflecting on this now, I realize that Jesus was in a similar predicament. It takes great courage to go against what your community considers absolute truth, which can lead to severe consequences. In Jesus's case, it led to crucifixion, while for others, it might result in facing a bishop's court.

At this point in my story, it's essential to address how I received answers to my prayers. Many of us might assume we learned how to receive answers to our prayers in Primary, but oddly enough, I never did. The crucial aspect for me was distinguishing a *no* answer from a *yes*. Understanding this distinction became essential for me in navigating my spiritual journey.

I had heard that a *no* answer manifests as a stupor of thought. This felt precisely as described: a mental haze or fog. For instance, if I thought, *I should call the bishop today to tell him I'm a practicing homosexual*, I would hold that thought in my mind to see how it made me feel. If, after a few minutes, I drifted off and struggled to remember the question, I would recognize it as a stupor of thought, indicating, to me, a *no* answer.

A *yes* answer starts the same way. I would ask the same question and would hold that thought in my mind. If I experienced a small rush of high energy and didn't forget the question, I considered that to be a *yes*. Sometimes a *yes* can be trickier than a *no*: if it's a soft *yes* or I'm afraid of the answer, I have a tendency to downplay it.

I would say to anyone else, practice. Ask a question you know the answer to, like, "Should I eat these sugary items — chocolate chip cookies, in my world — until I go into a coma?" Or "Should I neglect to visit a bathroom until after I have peed my pants?" Also, the word *should* needs to be dropped. It really works better to say, "Is it in my highest and greatest good to . . . ?"

I have great confidence in you. If you're new to this, simply practice and you'll get it. Also, everyone has a way of syncing with higher energy. Don't get stuck doing this my way. This is just what I used when I was looking for answers and didn't know any other way to go about it many years ago.

Also, you need to be very clear when asking your question. Don't expect the "powers that be" to read your mind. Be so precise that when you receive an answer, there is no doubt about what was addressed.

Additionally, ensure that you're energized when praying for answers. You should have some ability to stay awake: you'll think you are getting a *no* answer when, in fact, you're sleep deprived.

I think it was a November Fast Sunday that I was praying on my knees about whether I should confess to my bishop that I was a practicing homosexual. The answer felt like I had received an electric shock, a huge *YES!* I just said in my mind, *Let me get this straight. You want me to get up off my knees, go directly to the phone, and call my bishop to turn myself in. Right?* Another wave of intense high energy came over me. I just said, "Okay." I got off my knees, went to the phone, and called my bishop. At the time, I was the second counselor in the Relief Society presidency.

After I told my bishop I was gay, he was in shock.

He finally said, "You know what this means, right?"

"Yes, I know exactly what this means."

He said, "See you next Tuesday night at seven."

I just said "Okay" and hung up. I knew already that it meant we had just scheduled a bishop's court to determine whether I'd be disfellowshipped or excommunicated from the Church.

The Die Has Been Cast

When I finally called the bishop to confess my relationship with Ellen, I had been in the Relief Society presidency as second counselor for a year. I was the Young Women's president for three years before that and the second counselor in the Young Women's over the Beehives (twelve- to thirteen-year-olds) for five years before that. The point is, there was no way for me to just skulk away after being in such high-profile leadership roles. Also, I felt committed to live with my mom and didn't see myself going anywhere anytime soon.

Most gay Mormons I know just go "inactive" and stop going to meetings, or they move and leave no forwarding address. My patriarchal blessing said, "Ever resolve to never let a Church calling go unfulfilled." I was a pleaser anyway, so I had never been able to say no when called to fill a position in the Church. But with this caution in my patriarchal blessing, I was well and truly had. So, all I could figure to do was call and confess everything. That way, I would be off the "rolls" of the Church and not be harassed by anybody: home teachers and so on.

Nowadays, I hear you can resign from the Church without having to appear in person. But that wasn't an option for me at the time—at least not that I knew of.

With that one fateful phone call, I knew I had initiated a bishop's court. The "court of love," as faithful Church members call it, is where it's decided whether to keep you in the Church on probation (disfellowshipment) or to "throw you to the wolves" (excommunication). I may sound calm as I recount this now, but I was shaking when I set down the phone. From that fateful moment, I knew that my life would never be the same—for better or worse.

To explain further, I had many fears at that time. Without a doubt, I knew that I would lose my second family—the association with Church members in my ward—if I were excommunicated. Once you're out of the fold, frankly, you're unlikely to see them again, even when they're your neighbors. I did see a few of them in the grocery store afterward, but we were both uncomfortable and acted like we hadn't seen each other. When all this was happening, I had lived in that same house with my mom for thirty-four years. My second family and I had worked, served, laughed and cried together for over three decades.

I also feared that I would lose my job. My boss at that time was what I would call a superorthodox Mormon. He was so conservative that even the Mormons weren't sure of him, and one of his best friends was my current bishop. An excommunication is supposed to be very confidential. But my particular bishop had a reputation for being unable to curb his tongue. I worried that their confidential conversations would fill my boss with fear that my wickedness would rub off on his pristine business. And that would mean I could be fired.

My third fear was that my own family would reject me. For example, I don't know if I mentioned this, but one of my brothers-in-law happened to be my stake president at the time I made that fateful phone call. I knew he would be informed immediately. After all, he presided over my bishop. Would he tell my orthodox Mormon sister? I didn't know if my mom would disown me, not to mention my other siblings. The Church likes to have the saying "they abhor the sin but love the sinner." That's a fine line, and I wasn't sure how my life would change after the Tuesday night meeting.

The Court

I remember very little about what happened between Sunday evening and before the bishop's court on Tuesday evening, other than the fact that there was a dinner planned for that evening at my mom's house. It seemed like my older brother was going to be there with a friend or two. It wasn't a formal thing, but my mom and I were cooking and setting up for it. I remember being conflicted about what excuse I would give when leaving the dinner before everyone else left. I just told myself I would leave without explaining where I was going so no one would know of my meeting.

I'm sure Ellen must have known even though she wasn't at the dinner. I just remember dressing as if I were going to Church, excusing myself from the dinner, and driving myself to the Church house.

I went to the bishop's office and knocked. They were waiting for me: my bishop and his two counselors in the bishopric, one on each side of him. His secretary was there to take notes of the proceedings. All men, they were in dark suits with white dress shirts and ties.

And so the tribunal started. I was asked various questions and am sure the records show that I admitted to the heinous transgression of being a practicing homosexual. I almost said I wasn't a practicing homosexual because there clearly was no reason to practice. But I was wise enough to keep my smart-alec comments to a minimum.

Really, the one question that I clearly remember was this: "With all you know about the Church, how can you possibly reconcile what you know with this behavior?" I was one of those Mormons who enjoyed taking Institute classes at ASU, so the member of the bishopric who asked me that question assumed that I was highly knowledgeable.

I just said, "It's because I have more faith than you do."

The bishop said, "Excuse me?"

"Well, you all are on the point system," I said. "You give yourself a point for going to Church, a point for paying your tithing, a point for going to the temple, a point for doing your home teaching, and so on. You think that you might make it to the celestial kingdom if you have enough points. But Jesus knows the *integ-*

rity of my *heart*. I know that wherever I end up, there will be a party!"

This was a very unrepentant attitude, and I'm sure the tribunal didn't like it. But it was true. Christ came to throw out the point system and tell people that love is it. People, people, people, when will you stop counting and just care about each other? When will you stop judging and open your hearts?

Unsurprisingly, the bishopric and his secretary then excused themselves to decide what to do with me. They went into the next room while I waited. At this point, I didn't want to be disfellowshipped. I had already seen up front and personal what that looked like from watching Ellen go through it. I just wanted out.

When they came back into the room, they seated themselves. Then the bishop pronounced that the decision had been made to excommunicate me. It was a relief and a shock all at once. They told me I was not to wear Mormon underwear or garments, I couldn't pay tithing (not a considerable hardship), and I couldn't take the sacrament in Church.

All in all, though, it really was a relief. As I walked out the door, the bishop started telling me things I had to do. This was confusing because I figured that, since I was excommunicated, he and the Church no longer had jurisdiction over me. But when he got to the part where he said I could never have anything to do with my sweetheart, I'd had enough.

Knowing that the bishop adored his wife, I said, "Let me ask you something. If the Church said you had to leave your wife and you thought they were right, would you do it? But, more importantly, if they said you had to leave her, and you felt in your heart of hearts that they were wrong, would you do it?"

He stood there for a few seconds, not saying anything. But then he got red in the face and finally blurted out, "But mine is ordained by God!"

And I said, "How very lucky for you!" And then I walked out the door.

I realized later that the rules he was telling me about as I left the room were those that needed to be followed if I wanted to be rebaptized. The assumption is that all excommunicated people will want to get back in again. But I knew I was truly free—in a way I'd never been before. Knowing I could never go back to their tiny way of thinking, I was free to be who I was meant to be.

A New Beginning

So, dear reader, I did lose my second family immediately. It was awkward to still be living in the same house with my mom, seeing my neighbors but not really having anything to do with them.

I talked to my family members to let them know that I was gay and had been excommunicated. My mom was the first one I told because home teachers came to the house to give us the month's lesson. The "us" became just her since I was no longer on the rolls. She was unhappy with the outcome, but I think that had more to do with the fact that she felt it reflected poorly on her parenting skills.

But I still lived with her and really took care of household things. She could have thrown me out, but I was the best spouse she'd ever had in all ways but one. She was no fool. My sisters, to my relief, said that they loved me anyway. To me, that hadn't been a given, and I was grateful. My brothers had already pretty much broken from the Church, and they cheered me on too.

Ellen and I had been together for five years at the time I was excommunicated. She was excommunicated the same month I was because her year of probation had timed out and she hadn't repented—or dumped me. We were together for another sixteen years after that. So my initial thoughts that the relationship would last for, maybe, three months were a bit off.

And work was . . . Well, it kept on being work. My boss probably knew . . . Well, let's be honest, he did know. But I never once brought up the topic, and he didn't either. It was always the elephant in the room with us. As a matter of fact, I continued working for him at the CPA office for another fifteen years. Remarkable, really!

I clearly remember an experience I had after having been excommunicated for about six months. I was home one day when I began to feel a peculiar sensation inside my skull. I had never felt anything like it before and wasn't sure if I should be alarmed and go to the emergency room or just sit it out. It felt like someone had just poured milk (or water) on a bowl of Rice Krispies and my brain was going "snap, crackle, pop." At the time, I was a tad alarmed. Was I having prestroke symptoms or an aneurysm? Or just losing it mentally?

I thought, *Well, the worst case is that I'll just pass out.* But then this thought came to mind. My brain felt like it was a piece of roast that you truss up in string so it doesn't come apart in the roast pan. The strings had become rotten and weak and were just popping open one by one.

Then it occurred to me that my brain was finally free of all its constraints and was allowed to think anything that came before it!! "Pre-exing," I would stop my brain from thinking unallowed thoughts: like trying to figure out where the dinosaurs fit into the creation story. Or trying to figure out if God had made extraterrestrials to play a role in our world. But "post-exing," all thoughts were allowed. Maybe I still had to mull things over, but the fantastic thing was that everything was up for mulling.

My Way

I'm one of those people who place a very high value on integrity and authenticity. Not everyone does, and that's okay. My younger brother once told me, "You gave me great advice when I was younger. But you must understand that I couldn't take that advice because the only way I can 'get something' is to live through it. So your way, Sis, is not necessarily the right way. It's just your way."

That was a great teaching moment. My older brother never got excommunicated even though he had been actively gay since his twenties. I could never understand why he didn't just get out of the Church. But again, that was his way, and my way is just my way.

How interesting it is that our way, or your way, or anyone's way is just that. We so often think our way, or someone else's way, must be right. But the only thing that's right for you is what works for you. My brother even went on to say that if I'd had to live his life, I likely would have committed suicide. He is probably right. He's had an extremely stressful life. However, he said that he was fine with having gone through all the challenges he went through in his life.

He and I are built differently. I'm very sensitive and tightly wound. He isn't wired that way. What a help it would be if we could all just be right for ourselves.

So, if you're happy getting home teachers and being on the Church rolls, please continue to be happy. I trust that you're very good at taking care of yourself. But, if you are miserable and find yourself ducking down in the gay section of the bookstore as I did, it's all right to untangle your brain from all the "absolutes" you've been taught since you were in the womb. Not only is it all right, but for me, it was essential to reclaim myself.

Leaving the Fold

I don't think any of us "lifers" fully understand how much all the Church beliefs are intertwined with the very fabric of our lives. After I was excommunicated, I went to a counselor for a while to try to get more clarity on why I was feeling so lost. I do think it would have been more helpful to see a counselor of my same ex-faith. I went to a Jewish woman who was an excellent counselor, but she just couldn't seem to get her head around my struggle.

Despite that fact, I learned one important thing, which I have found to be true in my life: it takes a long time to rebuild a foundation, but the best thing you can do is trust your own intuition. That's what I did. Even from when I was in the Church, I could sense when something didn't sound truthful to me. Like when the lesson book said that obedience was the top law of heaven but I knew it was love.

I also knew that I didn't need another organization to fill the role the Church had played in my life. Friends were trying to tell me that I should go to their church, but I knew as soon as I walked out of the bishop's office that I never wanted to be coerced to believe in anyone else's set of beliefs. I also trusted my heart to tell me if a person or an organization was speaking the truth. There are times when the things being said sound exciting—when my ego likes how they sound—but they don't warm my heart. That's something I've have had to remind myself of over the past thirty years, and it still bears repeating.

I also knew that reconstructing my beliefs would take a while, and I was okay with that. I know that something that sounds groovy today may get thrown out tomorrow. My beliefs are flexible, and I love that about them. Every time I change my beliefs, I feel like this is it for now until I learn something better. None of my beliefs are carved in stone, but I feel good about them until something else feels better.

After I got out of the Church, I reflected on my journey and realized that the ability to change my beliefs was the core way I was able to get out of that huge programming with the least amount of trauma. If I had thought that my God was very disappointed in me and condemned me to outer darkness for being who I am, I would have been very depressed and angry. If I had thought life was a contest to see how valiant I could be, I would have had even lower self-esteem than I already had from being taught that we are to be perfect—whatever that definition is—even as our Father in heaven is perfect. If I had thought for a moment that I lost my God connection (Holy Ghost) because a group of men had judged me unworthy of that gift, I would have felt left at sea without an oar. But thankfully, I knew that all those thoughts were silly.

If I had thought that God wanted us to suffer, I would have been dismayed. If I had thought that God thought acting on my homosexuality was a heinous crime, I'm sure I would have been like those "other people" that I had met at Affirmation. If I had been shocked when I realized that I was a lesbian, rather than treating it as a matter of fact, it would have been one more reason to feel "less than."

But since my God loved the pity sakes out of me, made no judgments whatsoever, and wasn't impressed with any suffering, it was much easier to be cut free of that damaging belief system.

And right now, you may be thinking, "Sure, she can make up any fairy tale she wants to make herself feel better." But if you really think about it, all the stories that people repeat from old books are no better than the fairy tales people make up today. Everyone uses stories to better understand themselves, others and the world around them. And if the stories you tell yourself make you feel horrible for being you, why wouldn't you find a new story? What we haven't figured out yet is that what we have been told all our lives is just someone else's story that we've accepted as truth.

Similarly, I find it very curious that people think the only option they have if they reject their religion is to reject all notions of God. People assume that if they're not religious, they must be an atheist. That all-or-nothing mentality can be VERY limiting and unnecessary.

Rather than throw the baby out with the bathwater, why wouldn't you go within yourself and determine what qualities you need your God to have? For me, love has always been at the top. Always. Because of that foundation, I've found that I have felt supported and loved because all judgment is gone. Because my God never judges me or anyone else, I find myself less judgmental of both myself and others. Oh sure, we're all struggling right now trying to get along, but I have the profound knowledge that we are all good at our core. We are just in different classes taking the subjects our souls want to learn.

The thing that should be at the top of the list of truths is your own inspiration. No organization or person should be given precedence over what we know ourselves. Ever. We all are practicing becoming more aware of our inspiration.

This concept about knowing the truth inside your-self and accepting new stories that define how you view yourself and others became very evident after I had been excommunicated for a couple of years. One of the young women that I had been a leader of called and asked me to go by her house for a visit. At this point, she was newly married. I dropped by when she had asked me to. When we had gotten settled, she told me that many of the other young women for whom I had been a leader condemned me for being gay and getting excommunicated. She went on to say that she didn't feel that way about me. She said that she still loved and respected me.

I told her that I wasn't surprised about the other young women. But I did tell her that I wasn't bothered by what they thought of me. By that point in my life, I felt peaceful about my situation and really didn't care what others thought. I also told her that she had to be very mature and evolved spiritually to not judge me—or anyone else, for that matter—and that I loved and respected her too.

Epilogue

So, dear reader, did I leave anything out? The main thing I would hope you get from my experience is that I didn't become *one of those people* who were lost and angry. I am genuinely thrilled to be out. Were there challenges and adjustments to be made on the other side of being excommunicated? Of course there were. Did I go to a counselor for a while after that because it was rolling into December and I felt "cold" without my special underwear? Of course I did. I knew I was missing my traditions, but I also recognized my feelings of loss for my traditions for what they were and never for a moment wished to go back to that way of thinking.

Looking back, I know I've felt more spiritual being out than I could ever have felt when living a double life. I am free to just be me and to love just me. I am free to love in any way that my heart leads me. I have friends who are spiritual, like I am, but they're not religious. My God connection is better than it was because I "fired the white-male Mormon God" and got a God who is compassionate and has my back no matter what. How could my God not have my back since I am a part of God?

And lastly, to those of you who are struggling to find a way to be sane through this journey—which I did for five years—be kind to yourselves. Know that there are people before you on this journey, and there will be people after you who have this lesson to learn. Whether it's about the gay issue or simply clashing beliefs—I say "simply" as if it's less, which, of course, it isn't—know that *YOU ARE TRULY AMAZING*.

Whether you stay in the Church, like my brother, or get out, like me, you have my love and my respect. You are dismantling your programming. And that, my friend, can be very painful. May you know with absolute certainty that God is incredibly impressed with what you are doing. I'm impressed with that. You can only lose your God connection if you believe you've lost it. Please don't believe it because that would be a lie.

Hugs to you all,
Wanda

Acknowledgments

Sue Makinson Johnson held my hand throughout this process.

Brigham J. Taylor, my wonderful photographer, made me feel at ease in front of his camera. That's not an easy task.

Shelley Egan, my copy editor, edited every little thing so that, literally, I would look more correct than I am.

Justin Chevrier, my structural editor, filled in my blanks by asking me more questions about my life and times than I realized I had left out.

Ashley Russell, my artist and designer, brilliantly made my cover and the interior of my book come together.

Megan Williams is the mastermind behind The Self Publishing Agency Inc. She gave me direction and the hope that this book would eventually happen.

My sister Sharon Taylor supported me on my journey, even though she didn't want to know anything about my story.

David L. Payne, my brother, was my outside-the-box thinker. He started me thinking that I could write a book too.

My friend Judith G. Godell helped me with the initial editing of my book.

Lisa Treible, Karen Coda, Trina Berne, Judith Dean, Eric Heap, and Alan Payne—as well as others I may have forgotten to list here—gave me early and helpful feedback on my story.

Mormon Terms

Beehives — The young women in a ward who are ages twelve to thirteen.

Bishop — The leader of a ward. The bishop is always a male, and he has not been formally trained for this position. He has two counselors and a secretary. He is always chosen from the adult male members by the stake presidency.

General Conference — A worldwide, semiannual meeting led by the presidency of the worldwide Church and the Quorum of the Twelve Apostles. These men make up the guidance of the entire Church of Jesus Christ of Latter-day Saints (Mormons). Each April and October, on both Saturday and Sunday, there is one two-hour meeting in the morning and one two-hour meeting in the afternoon, for a total of eight hours of meetings. Then there is also a priesthood meeting on Saturday evening.

Patriarchal Blessing — A once-in-a-lifetime message given to someone who is a member of the Church. This blessing is meant to be a guidance for that member during their life. The blessing is given by the stake patriarch, who is ordained.

Relief Society — The organization that includes all the women in the ward from age eighteen and beyond. It has a president and two counselors, who organize the activities. Its focus is service oriented.

Stake — Stakes are organized from a group of contiguous wards or branches. To be created, a stake must be composed of at least five wards. A stake presidency (a president and two counselors) governs it.

Temple — Only Church members in good standing are allowed to go to the temple. Temples are where members can make sacred promises with God, including those related to marriage and family, and are believed to be a place of peace, learning and inspiration.

Ward — Congregations of Mormons are organized geographically, and members attend worship services near their home. Each member belongs to a ward or a branch (a small ward).

About the Author

Photographer: Brigham J. Taylor

Wanda was born and raised in Mesa, Arizona. She spent the majority of her career in the world of accounting and tax preparation. In her work, everything always balanced: black and white, debits and credits. But internally, she has always considered herself a healer, someone who seeks to help others find solace and comfort. An astrologer once told Wanda that she was an interesting combination of logic and feeling. When she decided to retire from much of her tax and accounting practice in 2024, it was time to write her stories.